Let's Make

GW01018621

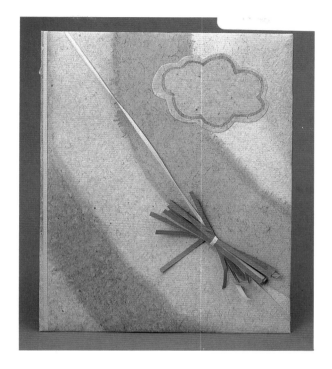

Juliet Crane

First published in 1994 by
BELAIR PUBLICATIONS LTD.
P.O. Box 12, Twickenham, TW1 2QL,
England

© Juliet Crane

Series Editor Robyn Gordon
Series Designer Richard Souper
Photography by Kelvin Freeman
Typesetting by Belair
Printed and Bound by World Print
Limited

ISBN 0 947882 48 0

INTRODUCTION

One of the most effective ways of encouraging children to write, and read, is to introduce them to the delights and many varied ways of creating a book.
This can be as simple as a zig-zag book, a scroll book, or four pages folded, sewn or stapled. It can be a spur-of-the-moment creation, or a long-term project; a gift for someone else, or a way of keeping a record for themselves; a personal diary, a nature diary, or a book of holiday memories.

Every book can include artistic input, both in the decoration of the cover, and the way the text is illustrated and designed. Very young children may produce a sequence of drawings, which can be a story without text, or which could be labelled by an older child, or an adult.

Some of the ideas will need assistance from an adult (especially where cutting is involved), but children will soon devise their own techniques, and variations on a theme - expecially when they have been introduced to all the possibilities of pop-ups, pull-throughs, zig-zags, flaps and shapes.

In the process of creating a book, children will be exercising their skills of language, art and design. The combinations of ideas are limitless, and those in this book can be seen just as a springboard for your own and the children's variations.

Juliet Crane

● We suggest that materials you would find very useful would be: a cutting mat (or wooden board), a craft knife (or small, sharp scissors), a long-handled stapler, a hole punch (or an awl for making holes), a large-eyed needle for threading wool, and fine ribbon - plus, of course, a good selection of paper and card.
● With a lot of the books or covers suggested in this book, it is important to weight them after they are made - for example, under a pile of books - so that they become, and remain, completely flat. This is especially important if the cover has required a fair amount of glue.

CONTENTS

ZIG-ZAG BOOKS

This is the simplest form of book, as it requires no stitching or attaching of any kind. Fold the paper concertina-style. As long as the length is quite a bit more than the width of the paper, it does not matter what size the paper is.

In the examples above:
1. The colour-labelled pictures were made by an older child for a younger child.

2. The mini-book is the story of a butterfly, told purely in pictures.
3. The story of the Treasure Hunt was first drawn, and then the text written separately, encircled by 'bubbles', cut out and added to the picture.

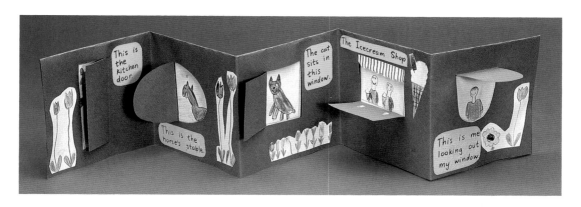

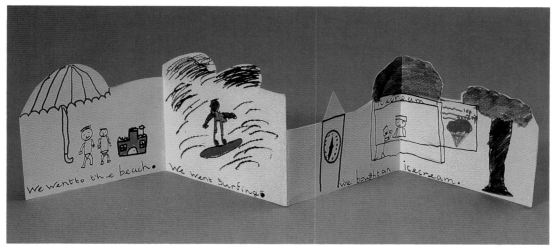

ZIG-ZAG BOOK WITH FLAPS

1. Fold a long rectangle of paper in half lengthways, then fold it concertina-fashion.
2. Open it out again and use a craft knife or sharp scissors to cut window and door flaps into each section. Refold.
3. Figures can be drawn directly into each window or door shape, or drawn separately on white paper and glued into place on the space behind the flap. The shapes of the flap will suggest certain types of use - e.g. stable, window, door, kiosk, etc.
4. Decorate the front of the zig-zag book with flowers, plants, signs, etc.

ZIG-ZAG BOOK WITH CONTOURS

1. Fold a length of paper concertina-fashion, then cut various shapes across the top of each section.
2. The shapes will suggest a certain landscape, or chain of events, and the picture and story can be written accordingly.
3. Children could cut the shapes themselves, or an adult could do this in advance.

● The story could, of course, be decided upon, written and drawn first, and then the contours cut out afterwards.

MIX-AND-MATCH BOOK

This can be great fun to make, and to share with others. It would not normally have text, but of course the various strips of paper could be labelled if you want.

1. Choose a piece of thick card for the back cover, and cut strips of paper for the pages, each one third the size of the cover. (The paper could be in different shades, as shown.)

2. Punch holes through the paper and card, and attach these to each other with binder rings, which can be bought in packs from stationery shops. (You could equally well use loosely tied wool or ribbon to thread through the holes.)

3. Devise lots of different heads, bodies and legs, and draw them so that they match up with each other and form strange combinations as the pages are turned.

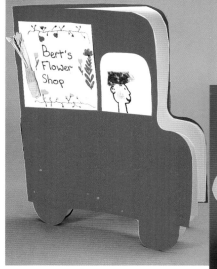

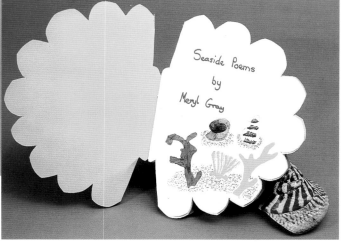

SHAPE BOOKS

These shapes were drawn specifically to tie in with class projects, but could be used equally well with an individual interest - a hobby, or a holiday diary, for example.

The Van Book

1. Fold a piece of red card, draw the shape of a van on the top half, and cut this out, making sure that the two halves are joined at the fold.
2. Fold several sheets of white paper in half to fit inside the card, trace around the van shape, and cut out the paper.
3. Staple, or sew, the cover and pages together.
4. Add the van driver and relevant details.

The Shell Book

1. Use a shell reference book and choose a shell to copy.
2. Fold card in half, draw the shell shape, and cut out, with the two halves joined at the fold.
3. Fold paper to fit inside the shell. Use the cover as a template, and cut out the paper the same size, or slightly smaller than the cover.
4. Make two holes on the fold line, and thread ribbon through to hold the pages together.
5. Decorate the shell appropriately.

SHAPE BOOKS

These books were made by an older child for a younger child (who added the illustrations).

ABC Book

1. On white paper, write the letters **'abc'** (in lower case) as 'bubble-printed' letters, and then fill in the shapes with 'Magic' felt-tip pens. (Each pen has a basic colour, which changes to another when drawn over with one particular pen.)
2. Cut out the **'abc'** shape, and glue it to a brightly coloured card, pre-folded so that it becomes the cover of the book.
3. Cut around the shape of the letters, leaving a border of the coloured card.
4. If you want a page for every letter of the alphabet, fold 13 sheets of very thin paper, insert these between the covers, use the cover shape as a template, and cut the paper accordingly.

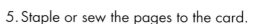

5. Staple or sew the pages to the card.
6. A letter of the alphabet can then be written on every right-hand page, and the pages illustrated accordingly.

Number Book

1. Make in the same way as the **'abc'** book, but using **'123'** for the cover design. Make an appropriate number of pages, depending on whether you want the numbers to go up to 10, 20, or above.
2. The number is written, and objects are drawn, on each page.

SHAPE BOOKS - HOUSES

Large Wallpaper House

1. Cut out a house shape, with roof, and space for garden, from a large piece of cardboard.
2. Use corrugated card, or painted card for the roof. Glue this on to the basic shape.
3. Cut sheets of wallpaper (maybe three or four - either left-over, or from a wallpaper sample book) to fit the house room shapes - making each piece about 2cm (or 1") wider than the house.
4. Turn this extra strip under on the left-hand side of each sheet and glue (each individually) under the edge of the house shape, so that the sheets turn like the pages of a book. (Adhesive tape could be used instead of glue.)
5. Decorate the garden, front of house

and rooms with scraps of fabric, and small drawings, to create details such as flowers, furniture, and people. The items can be labelled, or a simple story told about each room.

Small Front-opening House Book

1. Fold one piece of paper inwards so that the two flaps meet in the middle. Cut the middle section into a roof shape, and cut off the two side sections level with the roof. Draw tiles, or glue on a piece of corrugated card for the roof.
2. Rule lines to represent floor and walls, and draw the furniture, doors, windows, people, etc.

FABRIC BOOK

This is an ideal book for an older child to make for a younger child.

1. Cut long rectangles of fabric (at least twice as long as they are wide). Fold these in half, and sew at the centre fold.
2. Sew, or glue, the collage pieces on to each right-hand page to make the pictures. These could be individual pictures (not related to each other), or a series of pictures to tell a story.
3. Experiment with as many textures as possible - different types of fabric, fur fabric, net, ribbon, etc. Often the fabrics themselves will suggest a particular type of character or scene.

COLLAGE BOOK

1. Make the basic book shape with folded card, stapled or sewn.
2. Draw the figure outlines first, and choose fabrics with which to dress the figure.
3. Some of the fabrics may suggest certain uses, and help make decisions about what to put in the picture.
4. Add details, cut from fabric. In the examples shown here, one fabric pattern suggested grass, which was cut out and glued on, and pieces of a sunflower-printed fabric were added to the garden picture.

● Fabric shops often sell bags of remnants. For classroom use, parents could be asked to contribute remnants of fabric.

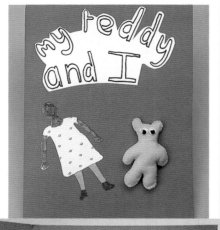

COLLAGE BOOK WITH A MOVABLE CHARACTER

This version of a collage book includes a movable character, who is transferred from the cover, and from page to page, as the story is read.

1. Fold several pieces of paper in half, and cut a coloured card cover in a slightly larger size. Either staple or sew the pages together.
2. Draw an outline of a teddy bear (or other character) on a piece of felt. Cut this out, together with an identical piece. Sew the two together and stuff with small amounts of cotton wool.

Add felt or button for eyes - or dolls' eyes from a craft shop.
3. Attach a piece of Velcro to the teddy's back.
4. Plan a story, choosing various ways of attaching the figure to the background (by using Velcro, or by slotting the figure into a pocket - as in the boat scene, and the bed picture).
5. Illustrations for the story can be a combination of drawn and collage pictures.

DIARIES - PERSONAL

Tied Diary

1. Choose two pieces of card for the covers of this book, and cut out two pieces of paper one inch larger all around than the card.
2. Attach the paper by gluing the edges under (having mitred the corners), and then neaten the inside of the cover cards by pasting another sheet of paper inside to cover the turned edges.
3. Cut the number of pages required (these can be added to later if necessary), slightly smaller than the covers.
4. Punch holes in the covers and pages and tie the two together with ribbon. Punch holes on the opening sides of the cover, and attach two ribbons so that the diary can be tied shut when not in use.
5. Decorate the outside of the diary with a picture.

'Keep Out' Castle Diary

1. Cut a piece of card, at least twice as wide as it is high.
2. Fold the short ends to meet at the centre, to form opening doors, of equal width.
3. Cut the shape of castle battlements along the two flaps, and add a figure of a soldier at the top.
4. Decorate the front of the castle and add a separate 'Keep Out' sign, hung over the battlements.
5. Staple sheets of plain paper inside.
6. Make a bolt for the door by gluing or stapling on a cardboard bar on one door, which slips through a vertical bar on the other door, and which is then secured with a third piece of card which slides through two slots on the first bar. These three pieces can be covered with gold or silver foil paper.

NATURE DIARY

This could be part of an ongoing project over several weeks or months, and can be an attractive collection of ideas, observations, photographs, line drawings and pressed flowers or leaves.

1. Choose a piece of corrugated card, or card in a natural colour, for the cover. It could be two separate pieces, or (as shown in the photograph) one long piece folded in half.

2. Cut paper to fit, and make holes (with punch or awl) through card and paper. Thread with string or raffia to bind the cover and pages together. Decorate the cover with a piece of torn paper and a pressed leaf.

3. Over a period of time, make observations about what is seen in the garden, the school ground or in the park, and note how changes occur during the seasons. Make a note of the birds seen, and the flowers and plants which are in flower at different times.

4. Press some flowers, leaves and grasses - having checked that the plants are not rare - and add these to the diary using strong glue.

5. Photographs can be taken of rare plants, or those which cannot be pressed. These are a vivid record of fleeting times in the garden, and are a good contrast to the more delicate drawings.

HOLIDAY DIARY

1. Collect together, while on holiday, such things as postcards, tickets, programmes, tourist leaflets, etc., and then add to this any holiday photographs and your own drawings.
2. Make a simple book - the one shown here was made with folded card, stapled at the centre using a long-handled stapler.
3. Decorate the cover, collage-fashion, to remind you of one of your holiday outings. The book shown here was decorated with a piece of fabric to represent a picnic cloth, and then the food was drawn and glued in place.

DECORATED COVERS

Torn Tissue Cover
1. Choose two pieces of tissue, in contrasting colours, and tear these into narrow strips.
2. Cut out your cover to whatever shape and size required, and cover the front with glue. Unless it is a very small cover, you may need to do this in small sections so that the glue does not dry before you use it.
3. Lay the pieces of tissue, overlapping, to completely cover the paper. Trim off the pieces which project beyond the edge.
4. Tear a small piece of gold or silver foil paper, glue this to the centre of the cover, and then attach a small drawing.
5. Press the cover overnight (under a pile of books) to make sure it remains completely flat, before adding the pages, sewn or stapled in place.

Clothes-collage Cover
Decorate pre-made books with collage pieces of paper (cut from magazines), fabric remnants, buttons, lace, etc. to represent clothes - ideal as a present for mother or father, aunt or uncle.

Rainbow-printed Cover
(See photograph on title page.)
The following technique is very simple, but the paper needs to be fairly substantial in order to take the wash of diluted inks without buckling.
1. Decorate the paper with a wash of water-based inks in rainbow hues, using a sponge or wide brush.
2. Make the books, stapled, sewn or bound.
3. Cut thin strips of paper in matching colours, tie these in a small bundle and attach with ribbon to make a bookmark.

FAREWELL BOOK

1. Collect together drawings from the people who are saying goodbye - and glue these to the front of your book, and write on a suitable message to the person leaving - perhaps a neighbourhood friend, a classmate or a teacher.
2. In the book put various things which will remind the person of what you have shared, and to let them know that they are going to be missed. These could include photographs, writing about what you have done together, postcards of the local area, reminders of sports events or school events that have taken place, etc.

MINI-BOOKS

Teddy's book
1. Make a book for a favourite toy or teddy - in the size appropriate for it. Make two holes and tie with ribbon.
2. Write a story in the book, and illustrate with tiny pictures.

Book in a Matchbox
1. Find a small empty matchbox.
2. Cover this with paper, glued on, with the join at the back. (Wrapping paper with a tiny pattern is ideal.)
3. Make a tiny book to fit inside the matchbox - the pages could be sewn together, or just folded and tied with wool.
4. Cover the little book with paper to match the box, and add a label.

Christmas Tree Books
1. Make very small books with card and white paper.
2. Punch a hole at the top left-hand corner, and tie ribbon through to make a loop.
3. Decorate the front with small Christmas drawings, embellished with glitter.
4. Use the books as decorations on a Christmas tree.
5. Inside could be written Christmas messages, or the words of Christmas carols.

'MY GALLERY' PORTFOLIO

1. Choose two large pieces of thick cardboard, and bind around the edges with tape. (In the example above brown paper tape was used.)

2. Punch two holes on each of the left-hand edges, and one on each of the right-hand edges.

3. Use ribbon or braid to match the edging tape, and use to make closures.

4. On the inside back cover make a pocket for your artwork by doubling a piece of thick paper and taping it on, using the same coloured tape.

5. Use the portfolio to hold your favourite pictures.

6. Decorate the front of the portfolio with a picture. Make a frame for this - the one shown was made with scraps of corrugated card. It could also be made with strips of scalloped foil, doilies, lace, or card sprayed silver or gold.

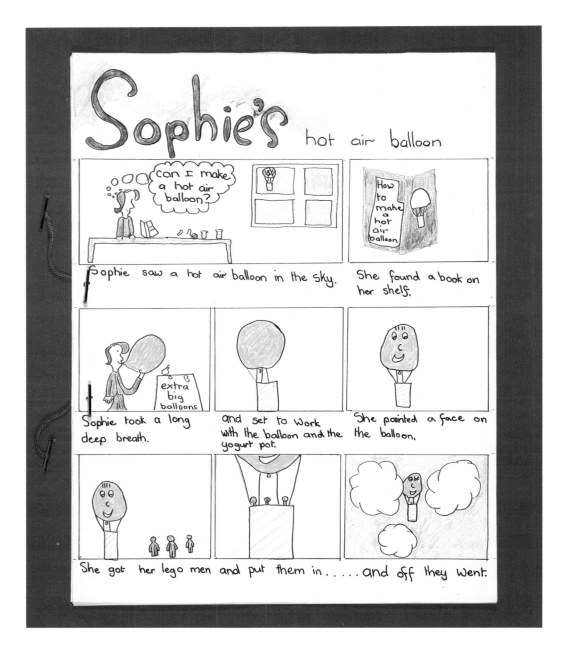

COMIC BOOK

1. Divide a page into sections.
2. Leave space for text under each picture, and/or use speech bubbles.
3. An ideal way to bind the comic strips together in order to add more, is to use tags as shown above - available from stationery shops.

● A very young child could make a smaller, simpler version, perhaps with drawings only - or with text added by an adult.

SCROLL BOOK

1. Cut a long strip of paper (lining paper is ideal), and you can trim off any not required when your story is completed.
2. Leave about 8" clear before your drawing and writing start, to allow space for rolling the paper later.
3. Speech bubbles can be used (as shown), written on separate paper,

and glued on afterwards, or the text written directly on the paper.

4. When the story is completed, cut off the paper at the end, leaving about 8" clear beyond where your pictures finish.
5. Glue each end of the paper around a cardboard tube from the middle of a kitchen roll.

FLAP BOOK

Magic Boxes

1. Make the book shape first, stapled or sewn, with an even number of sheets of paper to form the pages. Cut flap shapes in the first, third, fifth, etc. sheets.
2. Glue every set of two pages together so that the flap is on the front sheet, and the second provides a backing sheet when each flap is lifted.
3. Draw a box shape on each page, with the flap as the lid.
4. Decide what each magic box is going to contain - paint the pictures accordingly. These could be painted on separate pieces of paper and glued on, after decorating the backgrounds.

5. Use extra collage material to make the boxes more interesting (for example, the leaves and raffia nest shown in the photographs).
6. The text could be written directly on the page, or on separate paper, and glued on.

POP-UP BOOK

Completed pop-up pictures could be incorporated inside a simple sewn or stapled book, as long as the pages of the book are made from firm card.

Face Pop-up

1. Fold the piece of paper in half vertically, and draw a face on this. Cut around the face shape, leaving it uncut at about the ear level.
2. Fold the face section inwards so that when the page is opened the face stands forward. Add details with felt-tip pens, and scraps of paper for jewellery, etc.
3. Attach the background piece of the paper to folded card.

Pop-up Room

1. Fold a piece of paper in half and cut two parallel lines into the folded side to make the dressing-table. Fold this piece inwards so that it becomes the pop-up section when the page is opened.
2. Cut a chair shape in the same way, and, using a craft knife or small sharp scissors, cut out cat and vase shapes (left joined at the base). These can then be lifted up away from the flat surface, to add extra dimensions to the picture.
3. Lie the picture flat to decorate with felt-tip pens.
4. Attach the paper to a piece of folded card.

WORD-PROCESSED STORY BOOK

1. An older child could type a story himself/herself. A very young child could dictate a story to an older child or an adult. Word-processing gives very good experience in drafting, editing, adding to and extracting text.

2. The author can decide where the drawings should go, and spaces can be left accordingly.

3. The printed pages could be glued on to coloured sheets (as shown in the photograph) to give them extra body, and then the background sheets stapled or sewn together.

4. Word-processing gives an ideal opportunity to make extra copies of a story in order to share it with other people - parents, grandparents, friends, etc. Each book could be illustrated separately - or the first copy could be illustrated, and the others photocopied. The photocopies would usually be in black and white, but children have great pleasure in seeing their work reproduced.

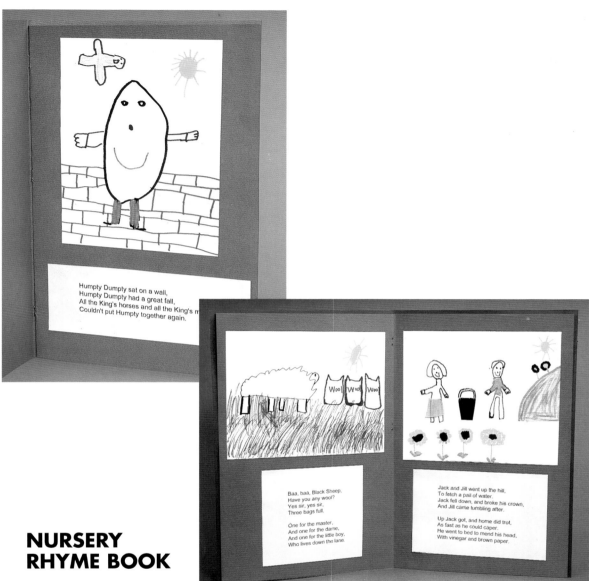

Humpty Dumpty sat on a wall,
Humpty Dumpty had a great fall,
All the King's horses and all the King's m
Couldn't put Humpty together again.

Baa, baa, Black Sheep,
Have you any wool?
Yes sir, yes sir,
Three bags full.

One for the master,
And one for the dame,
And one for the little boy,
Who lives down the lane.

Jack and Jill went up the hill,
To fetch a pail of water.
Jack fell down, and broke his crown,
And Jill came tumbling after.

Up Jack got, and home did trot,
As fast as he could caper.
He went to bed to mend his head,
With vinegar and brown paper.

NURSERY RHYME BOOK

An excellent reinforcement to the teaching of reading is the use of nursery rhymes which have already been memorised by the children. The rhyming words are particularly effective in helping children absorb patterns within written language.

For children just starting to read, there will be a great sense of achievement in being able to link spoken words with written words.

1. Choose rhymes that the child or children already know. Type (or write) these in large letters on individual pieces of paper.

2. Have the children illustrate each rhyme, and encourage them to read the rhymes to you and to each other.

● The rhyme books (or rhyme cards made in a similar way) could be kept, or displayed, in a place easily accessible to children.

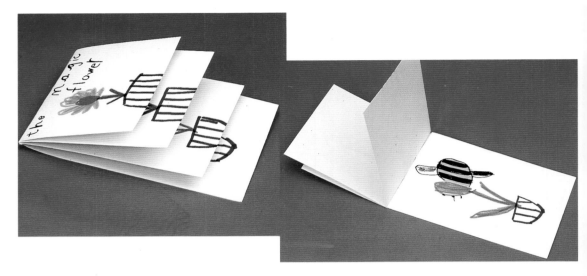

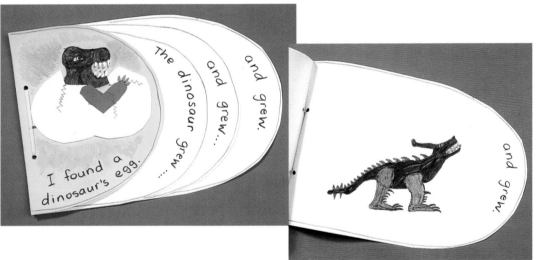

CHANGING SHAPE BOOKS

1. Staple or sew several pages of a small book together.
2. After securing the pages, cut them so that the smallest is on top, and the pages become progressively longer.

The Dinosaur Book

A book like this could be based on pure fantasy, or relate to a topic or specific interest, and show the stages in growth of a certain animal, or bird.

The Changing Flower

This could relate to the growth of a specific plant, or (as in the case above) it could be pure fantasy - showing how the flower changed gradually until it became a bee!

The shape of the book could, of course, be used in different ways, and the pages could become progressively smaller, or rounder, or change shape in a very fantastic way.

BOOK WITH POCKETS

This basic idea can be used in numerous ways, and here it has been used to hold some small gifts.

1. Make the basic book, either bound (see instructions on page 32) or, more simply, with pages and covers sewn or stapled together.

2. Make shapes from coloured paper to be glued on to the pages, forming pockets to hold the gifts.

3. Other gifts could be a poem, a comb, a sachet of handcream, etc.

4. Decorate the cover with drawings, and tissue collage.

BOOK WITH ENVELOPES

This concept is fascinating for children, who love receiving letters, and devising ideas for letters and envelopes. A favourite version of an Envelope Book is on the theme of Invitations.

The Invitation Book

1. Decide on the theme of the book - for example, 'Invitations to my party'.
2. Glue an envelope to each right-hand page, and write on each the name of the person (or animal) being invited.
3. On a separate piece of paper or card, made to fit the envelope, write the invitation.
4. Paint pictures of the guests, and write the corresponding text on the facing page.
5. Add party decorations to the page - paper balloons, small streamers made from cut and twisted crêpe paper, etc.

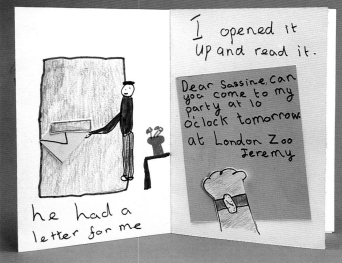

SLITS-IN-THE-PAGE BOOK

Suggest to the children that part of their story could involve a piece of paper being passed through from one page to the next. Let them imagine ways that this technique could be linked to a story, or how it could suggest a plot.

The boy who made the above book decided to draw a door, and have an envelope being posted through a letterbox - passing from one page to the next. He drew the door and the postman, and then he was helped to cut the letterbox flap so that an envelope could be passed through.

He then wrote the letter itself on a separate piece of paper, and drew a hand (which was cut out part of the way around) to hold the letter in place.

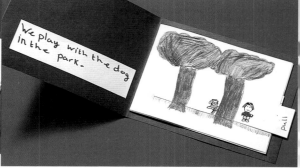

PULL-THROUGH BOOKS

There are many ways that this technique can be used. Once it is explained, older children can experiment and devise different ways of using the basic idea. A younger child can be helped to cut the slits and the moving card, and work out where to draw the figures.

1. In the park scene shown, the trees were drawn first.
2. Slits were made on either side of the trunks, and then a piece of card cut

which slid through behind the two trees.
3. With the Jack-in-the-box picture, the slits were cut at the top and bottom of the box, and a piece of card cut to slide through the openings.
4. Drawings were made (of the children in the park, and the Jack-in-the-box) so that when the card was pulled, they suddenly appeared or disappeared.

BOOK WITH HOLES

1. Make a book first with folded paper, and sew the pages together.
1. Paint, or make a collage, of a scene on the first page, and cut a hole in the page - using a craft knife, or small scissors.
Write text accordingly.
2. Decide what might be seen through this hole, and draw this on the second page, together with appropriate text. Cut another hole.

3. Continue on in this way - moving from one scene through to another.

● This can be a very good way of encouraging children to think creatively. For example, they could draw a picture of their own street, and then be asked, 'If there were a hole in that fence, what do you imagine could be on the other side?'

Binding a Book

1. Fold pieces of paper to make the book pages. Make holes down the crease mark, and sew the pages together.

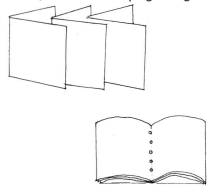

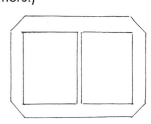

2. Cut two cardboard covers (just slightly larger than the pages) and lay these (about 1cm apart) on top of the piece of paper being used to cover your book - using glue spread thinly on the paper to keep the covers in place. (The covering paper should be large enough to allow about one inch all around for folding over. Mitre the corners.)

3. Put a small amount of glue round the edges of the paper and fold it over on to the card.

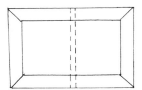

4. Apply glue to the first page of your sewn book, and place the book inside the cover, with the sewn edge in line with the centre of the spine of the book. Press firmly from the spine outwards to make sure the page is completely flat against the cover.

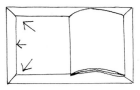

5. Repeat this with the last page of the book, gluing it firmly to the back cover.
6. Weight the book overnight, to make sure that the pages and the covers become completely flat.

For details of further Belair publications, please write to:
Belair Publications Ltd.,
P.O. Box 12, Twickenham, TW1 2QL, England.

For sales and distribution (outside USA and Canada):
FOLENS PUBLISHERS, Albert House, Apex Business Centre, Boscombe Road, Dunstable, Beds., LU5 4RL, England.